Gumdrop

Westfield Memorial Library
Westfield, New Jersey

W9-ACO-719

Westfield Memorial Library
Westfield, New Jersey

Westfield Memorial Library
Westfield, New Jersey

COMPETITIVE
GYMNASTICS
FOR GIRLS

Ann Wesley

J
796.44
Wes

Westfield Memorial Library
Westfield, New Jersey

Published in 2001 by The Rosen Publishing Group, Inc.
29 East 21st Street, New York 10010

Copyright 2001 by The Rosen Publishing Group, Inc.

First Edition

All rights reserved. No part of this book may be reproduced in any form without permission in writing from the publisher, except by a reviewer.

Library of Congress Cataloging-in-Publication Data

Wesley, Ann.
Competitive gymnastics for girls / by Ann Wesley.— 1st ed.
p. cm. — (Sportsgirl)
Includes bibliographical references (p.) and index.
ISBN 0-8239-3406-3
1. Gymnastics for girls. 2. Gymnastics for women.
I. Title. II. Series.
GV464 .W46 2001
796.44'0835'2—dc21

2001000057

Manufactured in the United States of America

Westfield Memorial Library
Westfield, New Jersey

Contents

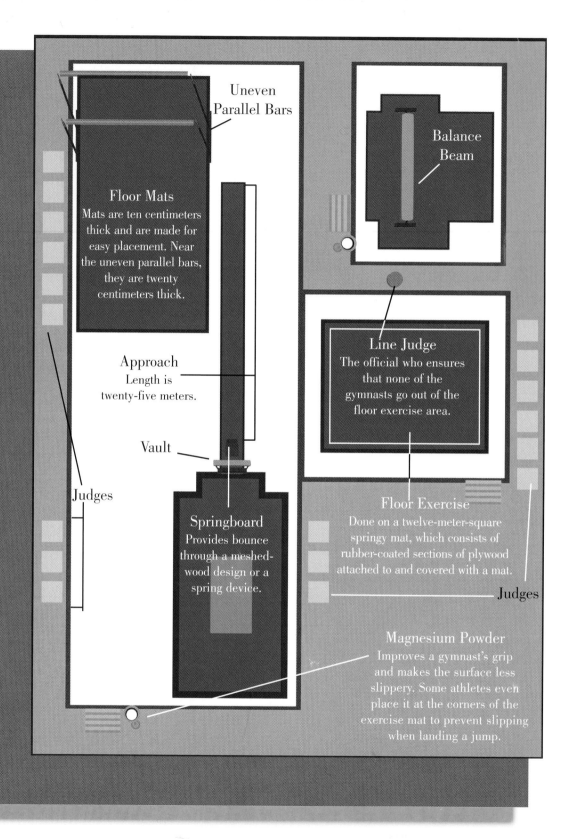

Uneven Parallel Bars

Floor Mats
Mats are ten centimeters thick and are made for easy placement. Near the uneven parallel bars, they are twenty centimeters thick.

Approach
Length is twenty-five meters.

Vault

Judges

Springboard
Provides bounce through a meshed-wood design or a spring device.

Balance Beam

Line Judge
The official who ensures that none of the gymnasts go out of the floor exercise area.

Floor Exercise
Done on a twelve-meter-square springy mat, which consists of rubber-coated sections of plywood attached to and covered with a mat.

Judges

Magnesium Powder
Improves a gymnast's grip and makes the surface less slippery. Some athletes even place it at the corners of the exercise mat to prevent slipping when landing a jump.

Introduction

A girl in a glittery leotard walks to the platform, passing the vaulting apparatus that is only slightly shorter than her four-feet, eight-inches. Her eyes are set in concentration. Her muscles bulge in her calves as she walks to the end of the runway. A tiny voice in her head echoes her coach's words telling her no one can beat her. She isn't competing against the other girls, she reminds herself. She's only competing against herself. She controls how well she will perform and thus what her score will be.

At the end of the runway, she signals to the stern-faced judges that she is ready to begin. She leans back then sprints toward the horse. Her feet land solidly on the springboard as her body flies forward. With her arms outstretched, her hands hit the horse and propel her upward, pushing her body almost perfectly vertical. While in the air her arms are outstretched as she maneuvers into a twisting motion, coming down facing the horse and the direction she came from. Her bare feet absorb the impact as she bends her knees to maintain her balance and keep from moving her feet. Steadying herself, she stands straight and puts her arms above her head in triumph. The landing is solid. The vault is a success.

The key to gymnastics, experts say, is doing something extremely difficult and making it look easy. There's certainly nothing easy about standing on a four-inch-wide piece of wood four feet off the ground, flipping your body into the air to twist and turn, and then landing perfectly on that beam without a wobble. And there's nothing easy about running at full speed, jumping on a springboard and vaulting high into the air to somersault twice and land without wavering. Yet when performed at the highest level, the sport looks graceful and effortless.

Women's gymnastics in its earliest form wasn't a sport. It combined dance and acrobatics and dates back to the days of the pharaohs. Gymnastics as a sport dates back to ancient Greece where men alone competed in the earliest Olympic Games. Thousands of years later, in the late 1800s, women began using gymnastics as a means of physical fitness. In 1928 they participated in exhibitions at the Olympics.

Competition as it is known today didn't really catch on until the 1950s, when gymnasts' individual skills were first judged in the Olympics. The first female gymnastics star was Hungarian Agnes Keleti. In the 1952 summer Olympic Games in Helsinki, Finland, she earned a gold medal in gymnastics floor exercise, a silver medal in team competition, and a bronze medal on the uneven bars. Four years later at the summer

Gymnasts don't just compete against each other. They also try to perform to the best of their own abilities.

Olympics in Melbourne, Australia, Keleti won another gold medal. In the same decade, Larissa Latynina and Vera Caslavska also made their marks on the world of gymnastics.

During the 1972 summer Olympics, the sport underwent an amazing transformation when a Soviet teenager named Olga Korbut stunned a worldwide audience by letting go of the high uneven bar, executing a half-backward somersault, and catching the apparatus on her way down. In another event, spectators were left equally astonished when Korbut performed a back flip on the balance beam—a common event nowadays, but then the first ever to be performed in competition.

Four years after Korbut's remarkable performance, she was almost overshadowed by another astonishing teen, Romanian Nadia Comaneci. Comaneci displayed such an extraordinary degree of grace and athleticism that she earned seven perfect 10.0 scores in the 1976 Olympics.

In the next two decades the sport of gymnastics moved from having a few women performing amazing feats to every serious gymnast working to make each routine more difficult, stunning, and dangerous. The perfect scores are still few and far between, but the goal remains the same. With each competition, whether it has been Mary Lou Retton dominating or Kerri Strug displaying triumphant courage, the bar of greatness is raised a bit higher and the skills become a lot harder to master.

This book will explore some of the basic principles of the sport and factors that motivate those who dedicate their childhoods to perfecting gymnastic skills.

Are Age and Body Type Important?

From the time a girl learns to crawl and walk, she often has an inherent interest in gymnastics. For most girls, that interest simply consists of turning cartwheels in the yard on summer days, taking early tumbling classes at a YMCA, or participating in cheerleading. Many leave gymnastics behind as they enter womanhood.

But for centuries, there have been women who never grew out of their love of gymnastics. Agnes Keleti was one of them. When she won that first gold medal in 1952, she was thirty-one years old, and when she won her second in 1956, she was thirty-five. Larissa Latynina and Vera Caslavska competed until they were thirty-two and twenty-six years old, respectively

But these women are rarely mentioned among the sport's greatest athletes. Their accomplishments have been overshadowed in gymnastics history by the performances of tiny teenagers such as Olga Korbut, Nadia Comaneci,

Mary Lou Retton was the first American woman to win the all-around gold medal in gymnastics.

Mary Lou Retton, and many modern-day athletes. Most of these young gymnasts retire in their early 20s or even sooner.

When these new stars showed the world that a four-foot-eleven-inch, 85-pound girl could perform daring, graceful, incredibly athletic moves on gymnastics apparatus and in floor exercise, the sport was changed, perhaps forever. Judges and coaches came to believe that to compete at the highest level and to maneuver their bodies in the way that these girls had, athletes had to be small. And the younger they were, the smaller their bodies usually were.

In 1956, when Keleti competed, the average U.S. gymnast was nineteen years old, stood five-feet, four inches tall, and weighed 124 pounds. By the early 1990s, the average age had dropped to sixteen, the height to four-feet, nine inches, and the weight to just over 80 pounds. Girls as young as twelve or thirteen were competing. The International Gymnastics Federation realized that such fierce competition wasn't healthy or safe for girls who were still growing. In 1996, the federation stated that a girl had to be fifteen years old to participate in world competition. In 1997, the minimum age for women's gymnastics at a world championship or the Olympics was raised to sixteen.

But more important than age in the sport of gymnastics is body shape and size. Female bodies are generally divided into three types: heavy, thin and muscular, or slim. Most girls do not fit one type exclusively. But the unique body type a girl has may determine which events in gymnastics she will have a better chance at mastering. For example, those girls with a combination body leaning toward a heavier shape and size often are more successful in balance beam because of a lower center of gravity. Girls with thin, muscular shapes often excel in routines on the vault or uneven bars that involve flipping and twisting the body over quickly.

The fact that many of the gymnasts in international competition are tiny doesn't mean that only small girls can enjoy the sport. Just as a four-foot-eleven inch, 85-pound girl would need spectacular skills to play professional basketball, a six-foot-two-inch, 176-pound girl is not likely to be a top-ranked gymnast. But any girl who works hard can accomplish other goals in gymnastics. Walk into any gymnastics school or sporting event and you'll see girls from preschool to college age—and older women as well—performing gymnastic skills in competition, for fun and as part of cheerleading, dance, and other sports. Nowadays, more than two million people in the United States participate in gymnastics. In 1999, the National Collegiate Athletic Association (NCAA) listed ninety-one schools at the college level offering gymnastics programs in Divisions I, II, and III. Only a handful of gymnasts make it to the international level. For the rest, the sport provides exercise, enjoyment, and competitiveness.

"I think it's possible to be five-feet, nine-inches and be a good gymnast," said one fourteen-year-old competitor, standing just five-feet, one-inch. "That's just my personal opinion. It might affect you slightly, but you can overcome it. Tall gymnasts look more impressive doing the same skills. It just means you might have to work harder." A gymnast's mother adds, "Being small makes it easier to make fast rotations because your body mass tends to be in tighter to center."

Many coaches believe the best age to start a girl in gymnastics training is between two and four years old. At that age, children are naturally interested in tumbling and are still developing their sense of self. They usually don't have the fears of falling or getting hurt that older students can have. Beyond that starting level, girls enter classes, not by age, but by skill level. Beginner classes teach the basics and let the students begin more extensive work on the balance beam, uneven bars, vault, and different floor exercises. When a girl is ready, she moves to the intermediate or advanced levels where a set of skills is put together into a continuous routine.

If a girl decides to move into competition, she will be evaluated and placed in a skill division from 1 to 10. Competition levels range from 5 to 10, with

Girls with heavier bodies do well on the balance beam because they have lower centers of gravity.

Gymnasts who want to compete must work long and hard to develop skills such as balance and strength.

those reaching the top moving on to the elite or Olympic level. Many communities support strong level 2 to 4 programs through Amateur Athletic Union (AAU) organizations.

When a girl moves into the upper levels of competition, she usually needs to make a serious commitment to gymnastics, sacrificing some of her social activities to focus on practice several times a week. Sometimes a gymnast spends as much time practicing as she does in school! She learns lessons in anatomy, balance, sports medicine, and the laws of gravity. Gymnasts train their bodies to stretch and hold positions for several minutes. They learn to combine dance with athletics and maneuver their bodies around equipment, and they practice each move until it's perfect. While athletes in other games can still win after making mistakes—dropping a fly ball in softball or missing a jump shot in basketball—one tiny mistake in gymnastics will not only knock the athlete out of competition, it can result in serious injury. In 1998, a Chinese gymnast, Sang Lan, was left paralyzed after she fell during a practice session for that year's Goodwill Games.

One twelve-year-old gymnast spends about eight hours a week in the gym. She's been with the sport just a year. She knows she'll never make it to the Olympic Games, but still enjoys her sport. "I really started too late to be an elite. I'm practically the only one who is twelve and still on level 4. I don't care, though. It doesn't matter how old you are, how tall or short you are, how good you are. If you are having fun, then that's what counts."

Building Strength

Normal, everyday activities may be enough to build strength. In other cases, a coach may incorporate sit-ups, push-ups, chin-ups, and other exercises in the training. And in some cases, weight lifting may be incorporated. No exercise program should be started without the advice and assistance of a trained professional. Doing these activities the wrong way can result in muscle strain or serious injury.

Some basic strength exercises include:

Simple push-ups (sometimes called girls-style push-ups): Lie on your stomach, legs together and arms bent so that your hands rest, palms down, on the floor next to your shoulders.

Bend your knees and point your feet up. Push your body up until your arms are straight. Your back should stay straight and knees must stay on the floor. Lower your body back to the floor and repeat.

Leg squats can help improve your balance.

🛑 **Push-ups:** Similar to simple push-ups but do not bend the knees. Put your toes on the floor and push your entire body up, keeping your back and legs straight. Some doctors don't think this move is safe for girls.

🛑 **Leg-squat:** Stand on one leg with your arms pointing out and your other leg held straight out, parallel with your arms at about hip level. Squat down on one leg and slowly stand back up, keeping your non-support leg held straight out.

You can hold on to a chair to help keep your balance. Switch legs and repeat.

🏋 **Press:** Stand with legs spread shoulder-length apart. Bend over straight and put your hands flat on the floor about eight to ten inches in front of you. Shift your weight onto your hands by raising up onto your toes and shifting your hips over your shoulders. This will build strength and help you develop a solid handstand.

Building Flexibility

The more flexible her muscles become, the better range of motion a gymnast will have. However, there's a danger of muscles becoming too loose and, as a result, more open to injury. The younger a gymnast is, the easier it is for her to become flexible, but proper exercises and stretching can enable almost anyone to become more flexible. The important thing to remember in any flexibility exercise is to move in a controlled manner rather than a fast, jerky way and to ease into the stretch rather than push through a point of pain.

Some basic flexibility exercises and stretches include:

🏋 **The split:** Start by standing with one leg in front, bent at the knee, while the back leg stays straight.

Lean forward until you can put your hands on the floor on each side of the front foot. Slowly push backward with your back leg until your front leg is straight. Slowly take some of the weight off your hands. With practice you will be able to get all the way down. Reverse position and split with the back leg in front this time. As you become more comfortable with this position, you will learn a right split (facing right); left split (facing left), and middle split (facing forward).

Back arch: Lie on your back, with your knees bent and your feet together tucked as close to your bottom as possible. Put your palms flat on the floor next to your shoulders with your thumbs pointing at your ears and your fingers pointing down toward your body. Using your arms, push up until your arms are straight. Then push up with your legs so that your whole body is arching like a bridge while your hands and feet stay on the floor.

Hamstring stretch: You'll need a partner for this one. Each girl sits facing the other as they press the bottoms of their feet together with legs together and stretched full out. Reach forward and hold hands, holding this position for several seconds. Hold the right hands, then left, then both.

Gymnasts help each other do the hamstring stretch to improve their flexibility and range of motion.

When proper strength and flexibility movements have been learned, it's time to learn some basic skills.

Basic Skills

Forward Roll

This basic somersault must be mastered before you can go any further in gymnastics. Squat and rest your chin on your chest. Tuck your body into a ball, lift your rear end, and roll forward. End the move in the same squat position you started with. Be careful not to roll with such force that you drive your head into the mat. Keep your knees pulled in against your chest and close to your head.

Backward Roll

Squat in a ball with your arms against your sides and bent so the palms of your hands are next to your shoulders and facing up. Rock backwards, staying tucked in a ball, and push against the mat with your hands to push over. End back in the squat position. You must roll fast and hard.

The Cartwheel

Stand in an X-shape, arms and legs apart. Imagine a clock with your arms at 10:00 and 2:00 above your head. Your feet should be at 8:00 and 4:00. Keep your eyes set on the mat on the position you will hit and move in a straight line. If you start with your left foot out, then put your left hand out. If you start with the right foot, put the right hand out. Step forward and lunge with the leg, bend at the waist, and reach towards the mat with your hands while driving your back leg over your head. Land with your kick leg first, push with your hands, bring the other foot down, and stand. Your movement should be hand, hand, foot, foot.

The Handstand

This is a skill needed for most events and one of the first moves that must be mastered. It is important to not only be able to get into a straight handstand position, but to be able to hold that position for a minute or more. You see versions of the handstand in floor exercise, balance beam, and gymnastic routines.

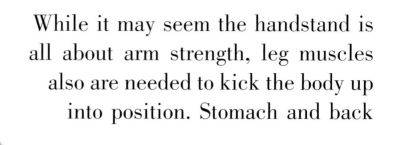

While it may seem the handstand is all about arm strength, leg muscles also are needed to kick the body up into position. Stomach and back

muscles are needed to keep the body in the proper position. One of the first things to learn is how hard to kick to get your body upright without having too much momentum and going all the way over. Many gymnasts recommend doing handstands against a wall with your back and feet against the

Handstands are needed for most events, so you must master this skill to be a gymnast.

wall. Once in the handstand position, hold steady for as long as you can—starting with several seconds and gradually building up to a minute. As you get better and stronger, you can move away from the wall and rely on your strength alone to hold you up. Whenever you begin doing handstands away from the wall, it is important to have a spotter with you to make sure you don't fall and get hurt. A spotter should be strong enough to catch you and know enough about your sport to offer constructive advice.

To prevent bad habits from forming, some common mistakes should be avoided while learning handstands.

- Never place your hands wider or narrower than the width of your shoulders.

- Never arch your head back or forward.

- Always keep your stomach and middle of your body straight.

- Always keep your legs together and straight.

Equipment

Women's gymnastics revolve around four basic events: balance beam, floor exercise, uneven bars, and vault. With the exception of floor exercise, each event involves a piece of equipment or apparatus. The floor exercise is performed on mats and the skills used there are carried into the other events. What follows is a description of each event and the skills needed to perform within it. Each gymnast will naturally have her favorite, but to be an all-around gymnast, action in each event is needed.

Floor Exercise

This is performed on a special mat measuring forty feet long and forty feet wide. Under the mat is a spring-enhanced floor. Gymnasts perform their floor exercise to music and use the entire mat area to showcase tumbling and dance skills. Gymnasts must not step outside the boundaries of the mat and generally must complete a specific set of skills within ninety seconds. This doesn't give a girl much chance to think about her moves.

Typical skills used in the floor exercise are tumbling interspersed with leaps, jumps, twists, turns, and dance moves. As with other routines, the action must be continuous and smooth. The gymnast must have excellent body control and make her skills look effortless.

Balance Beam

This is a sixteen-foot long piece of wood that is four inches wide, set in a stand four feet high. When gymnasts perform on the beam in competition, they must use the full length of the beam and must perform for one minute to a minute and a half. The routines must cover specific skills such as moving from a standing position to a kneeling or sitting position and getting back up smoothly. The most important elements of this event, other than staying on the beam, are demonstrating power and control while performing a smooth, diverse routine that includes peaks or high points of skill. These peaks generally consist of putting two or more moves together in quick succession such as a cartwheel, a back handspring, and a back flip.

The secret of a good beam performance is to keep your center of gravity over the beam at all times. This means the hips and shoulders must be square to the beam. Your feet should be turned out slightly and your toes can grip the side of the beam to help balance. You should not be watching your feet—instead, you should keep your head up.

Uneven Bars

The uneven parallel bars are two bars of different heights suspended in a metal frame. They can be adjusted for each girl, but the low bar must be 148 centimeters tall, plus or minus 3 centimeters, while the high bar must be 228 centimeters tall, plus or minus 3 centimeters.

The object of the event is to swing around the bars and move from one to the other in a smooth, strong rhythm without stopping. A gymnast must have the courage and strength to let go of the bar, perform a skill, and catch the bar again. She must change handgrips many times and must incorporate big moves in with graceful swings. The gymnast must stay in complete control of her body so that she can stop the action, hold a move, and reverse direction. At the end of the routine, she must perform a tumbling dismount and land on steady feet.

A gymnast must be strong and brave to compete on the uneven parallel bars. She has to let go of the bar, perform a routine in mid-air, and then catch the bar again.

Gymnasts use chalk (magnesium carbonate) on their hands to reduce the friction between the palms and the surface of the bars. Gymnasts who work out a great deal on bars may use leather handgrips on their palms to reduce friction and provide a more stable grip on the bar.

Vault

Vaulting consists of a strong, fast run down a runway that measures one meter wide and no more than twenty-five meters long, with a springboard and a padded "horse" at the end.

Don't Let It Rip

In many sports, letting something rip is a good thing—it means go for it or give it your all. In gymnastics, a rip is not a good thing. A rip is a tear in the skin caused by blisters that break open. This is most common in uneven bar work because of the friction against the hands. Girls will generally develop calluses and some will use anything from lotion to leather grips to try to keep hands protected, but rips are a part of this sport.

When a rip occurs it must be treated properly to prevent infection. The open blister should first be washed with soap and warm water and dried. Soap may burn, but it is needed to clean the wound. The ripped area should then be bandaged and taped. If you don't have to continue practice, don't. If a rip happens during a meet or you need to continue practicing, make sure the area is taped properly so the tape doesn't roll up and cause more problems. After practice apply an antibiotic ointment and keep the area clean and covered until it heals. If there are any signs of infection, see a doctor immediately.

It is vital for a gymnast to get a strong running start when doing the vault, so she can jump on the springboard with enough power to contact the horse.

The vaulting horse stands 120 centimeters tall and is 35 centimeters wide by 160 centimeters long.

The gymnast runs down the runway, then jumps on the springboard to give her enough power to make contact with the horse with her hands, timing it so that she can hit an exact spot, while her feet fly over the head. Pushing off the horse, she manages flips, twists, somersaults, and other acrobatic moves before landing on steady feet.

Vaults are grouped into four categories:

1. Forward approach vaults in which the body flips over to land facing forward. Flips are optional.

2. Forward approach vaults with a flip in landing flight. This involves a backward or forward flip to land.

3. Vaults with a turn onto the horse and a flip in landing flight

4. Vaults (with or without flips) from a round-off onto the springboard.

A common fault in vaulting is having the arms positioned above the head while the feet are still on the springboard. The arms should come from behind and lift up and forward during the jump and takeoff (except with round-off entry vaults). Girls should practice this on the floor before moving to the vault.

Scoring

Gymnastics competitions are judged and scored both as individual and team events. Each girl is required to perform a required number of specific moves on each piece of equipment. Points are awarded on a scale of 0 to 10 for each event, with 10 being a perfect score. Judging is subjective; that is, each judge has his or her own opinion of how well the skill was performed. There are guidelines for judges to use to try to make sure the scoring is fair, and judges must be very knowledgeable about the sport but, unlike many other sports, the score is based primarily on the opinion of the judges. Usually there are four judges, and the highest and lowest scores are dropped to provide a more objective total score. There are two types of routines in gymnastics—compulsory and optional.

Compulsory

In the compulsory routines, each gymnast must perform a required set of skills. Each skill must be executed in a specific order with the correct height, timing, and body position. Judges start scoring at a perfect 10 and make deductions for each type of error detected.

To achieve a solid performance on the beam, a gymnast must keep her center of gravity over the beam at all times.

Optional

In the optional routines, there are basic skills to be performed but they can be executed in different styles that make them more or less difficult. The difficulty ratings are regularly changed by the International Gymnastics Federation as the sport evolves and athletes continue to add harder and harder skills to their routines. In judging the optional routines, the score begins with a possible 9.60. Up to 0.40 can be added based on the level of difficulty of the routine to make a perfect 10. As with compulsories, points are also subtracted for errors. The degree of difficulty a routine carries is determined prior to the event so that each judge does not individually decide how difficult the routine is.

3 Safety

Before any gymnast first gets on the balance beam, grabs the uneven bars, or touches the horse, she must be able to perform the routine. Trying to learn the moves on a specific piece of apparatus will most often lead to serious injury. Many hours must be spent learning moves and mastering skills in a protected setting with a trained, experienced teacher or coach before trying them on your own.

While parents may want to help a girl learn gymnastics and may volunteer to 'spot' a daughter, that decision is unwise if the parent is not trained. A proper spotter knows how to guide the athlete through a move and is strong enough to support the gymnast. In the early stages of learning, the spotter may actually carry the girl through the motion while telling her how and where to place her hands, arms, legs, and feet.

One type of spotting device involves a belt with ropes attached through pulleys. The coach uses the ropes to lift a gymnast and help her through a routine.

Some gymnastics schools use a belt with ropes attached through pulleys as a spotting device. The coach can use the ropes to lift the gymnast and help her maneuver through the routine. Other schools may use a landing pit, which is basically a large rectangular hole cut in the floor and filled with soft landing mats. It helps beginning gymnasts to know they will land on a safer surface.

When it comes to actually learning the gymnastics moves, a girl must realize that this sport cannot be learned after only five minutes of instruction. To become a good gymnast, an athlete must put in several hours of work each week in addition to undergoing strength and flexibility training. While younger girls often have less fear of tumbling or trying new skills, they often lack the attention span and discipline needed to participate in gymnastics.

Before attempting any routine, a girl and her coach should make sure she is strong enough. Before performing it on a piece of equipment, such as the balance beam, the gymnast should be able to perform the trick perfectly on a straight line on the floor. She should honestly decide whether she is nervous about doing the skill. If the answer is yes, she is likely not ready to try it on a piece of equipment yet. She should also take the time to mentally prepare for the skill. Many coaches say a skill must be performed eighty to a hundred times before it is "programmed" into the brain and the gymnast's body is trained to do the move.

Visualization is one of the primary elements of preparation in gymnastics. In order to understand the skill, a girl must be able to see herself doing it and then be able to describe it clearly. If she can't describe in her own words what she will do, she may not have a clear understanding of that specific skill. Before attempting the move, the girl should be able to tell the coach what position her arms and legs and body should be in during any part of the skill.

It's important not to try to take on too much at one time. Learn a skill, master it and then add new things. If you try to learn too many skills at one time, you'll have a basic knowledge of many, but not be able to perform any well.

Each gymnast moves at her own pace. You should feel pressure to improve your performance, but you shouldn't feel fear. If you are afraid to try something, it's often a signal that you don't understand the move or haven't mastered the skills you need.

So how do you know when you are ready to move on? One rule of thumb is to count how many times you do a move correctly in a practice session. You should perform the skill correctly on more than half of the attempts you make before you decide to add harder elements to it.

In gymnastics, as in any other sport, injuries are going to occur. A gymnast can take steps to reduce the chance of injury—using a spotter, understanding a move, stretching, staying focused—but sometimes the nature of the sport is going to lead to injuries. The American Academy of Orthopedic Surgeons reports that each year physicians treat more than 86,000 gymnastics-related injuries.

It is important for a young athlete to understand whether a pain is the result of normal activity or the result of an injury. When a gymnast first becomes involved in the sport some degree of pain will almost certainly occur as muscles are stretched and used in a new way. That pain, though, is different from the more severe pain caused by an injury. When an injury occurs, gymnastics activity should stop until the injury can be assessed and a professional can advise whether it is safe to continue.

Before trying a new routine, a girl and her coach should discuss whether she is strong enough and mentally prepared for the challenge.

Canadian gymnast Emilie Fourner grimaces as she has her ankle examined by a doctor after injuring it while practicing her floor routine. Sprains, muscle strains, and stress fractures are common—and painful—injuries in gymnastics.

Sprains are among the most common injuries in gymnastics. A sprain is a pulling or a tearing of a ligament connecting the bones at a joint. The intensity of the sprain can range from mild to severe. The more severe the sprain, the less likely it is the ankle will hold weight. The ligament may become partially or completely torn in severe strains and will need to be treated by a doctor. Minor sprains can be treated with ice to reduce swelling and rest. The most common areas of sprain for gymnasts are ankles, wrists, knees, and backs.

Muscle strain is another common ailment for gymnasts. A muscle strain may occur when you overstretch or tear a muscle or tendon. Strains can usually be treated by resting and applying ice to the sore area. More severe strains may require a visit to the doctor.

Muscle soreness is inevitable in gymnastics and most other sports. Many times the pain doesn't set in until a couple of days after a hard workout. This is known as delayed onset muscle soreness. In normal exercise, tiny muscle fibers can tear when pulled, causing pain. These fibers will, however, rebuild in a day or two. This type of injury can usually be prevented by stretching well before and after exercise and by gradually working into a hard routine instead of going all out two minutes after entering the gym.

A more serious injury that can affect gymnasts is a stress fracture. This injury typically occurs because of continuing overuse of a joint. The main symptom of a stress fracture is pain. The most frequent places a stress fracture occurs are the leg bones and feet. Depending on the severity of the injury, treatments include rest, wearing a cast, and physical therapy.

Following these safety guidelines can help you prevent injury and enjoy your sport.

Always stretch before starting a workout. Hold each stretch for at least thirty seconds.

Always use an experienced spotter. A coach should spot gymnasts during all practice sessions when complex or challenging routines are being performed.

- Check the equipment to make sure it is properly maintained.

- Make sure proper mats are being used and that they are placed correctly to pad landings.

- Avoid loose-fitting clothing that can get caught on equipment.

- Stay focused. An interruption in concentration or unnecessary distraction can cause a fall and lead to injury.

Eating Disorders

In any discussion of gymnastics and safety the issue of nutrition and eating disorders is always a concern. According to a 1992 American College of Sports Medicine study, eating disorders affected 62 percent of females in sports with an emphasis on being thin, including gymnastics. In gymnastics, points are awarded for the routine—but unfortunately, the athlete's appearance and body type still can influence judges.

The two main eating disorders affecting gymnasts are anorexia nervosa and bulimia nervosa. An anorexic condition consists of significant weight loss from excessive dieting. Anorexics often consider themselves overweight and try to avoid eating, even when their actual weight is well below medical standards. Like anorexia, bulimia is characterized by the desire to be thinner, even when a girl may already be underweight. But rather than an avoidance of food, bulimia involves binge eating—frantic overeating—following by forced vomiting or the overuse of laxatives. Those affected by either disease often suffer from low self-esteem, have a strong desire to be the best, and desperately want to please others.

For active athletes, not eating enough does not provide the body with enough energy to get through a routine or practice. Girls become lightheaded and unbalanced and can faint. Long-term effects of eating disorders include organ failure and cardiac arrest. Gymnast Cathy Rigby, an Olympian in 1972, battled eating disorders for twelve years. Twice she faced death when she went into cardiac arrest. In the 1980s, elite gymnast Christy Henrich was told she was too heavy to be the best. In attempts to control her weight, she developed anorexia and bulimia. She died in 1994 after her weight dropped to only forty-seven pounds and her organs failed.

Warning signs of anorexia nervosa can include noticeable weight loss, excessive exercise, fatigue, depression, cold hands and feet, muscle weakness, obsession with food, regular excuses for not eating, unusual eating habits, discomfort around food, complaints about being fat, cooking for others but not eating, mood swings, irritability, evidence of vomiting, use of diet pills, irregular menstruation, fainting and dizziness, being secretive about eating habits, pale or pasty complexion, headaches, and low self-esteem.

Warning signs of bulimia can include binge eating, secretive eating, bathroom visits after eating, vomiting, use of laxatives and/or diet pills, weight fluctuations, swollen glands, broken blood vessels, excessive exercise, fasting, mood swings, depression, low self-esteem, self-worth determined by weight, negative thoughts about self after eating, fatigue, muscle weakness, tooth decay, irregular heartbeat, avoidance of restaurants or social events that involve food, and substance abuse.

Anorexia and bulimia can be treated with the help of therapists, doctors, and nutritionists. Gymnasts and those around them should be aware of the above warning signs of eating disorders. Gymnasts should only diet with the advice of a professional.

4 The Future

In 1972, Congress passed Title IX of the Education Amendments of 1972. It states, "No person in the United States shall, on the basis of sex, be excluded from participation in, be denied the benefits of, or be subject to discrimination under any education program or activities receiving Federal financial assistance." Since its passage, girls have been given more opportunities to participate in sports. In recent years the explosion of female participation in sports has been so dramatic that the days of girls standing on the sidelines watching or performing just for pure entertainment value are long gone.

In 1997, "Physical Activity and Sport in the Lives of Girls," a report of the President's Council on Physical Fitness and Sports, stated the importance of providing more opportunities for girls in sports and increased community efforts to help more females get involved in physical activities.

The President's Council report found that:

- Girls' early involvement in physical activity and sport can reduce their likelihood of developing a number of chronic diseases and unhealthy conditions, such as coronary heart disease and high cholesterol.

- Regular physical activity can help girls build greater peak bone mass, reducing adult risk of osteoporosis.

- Exercise and sport participation enhance mental health by offering adolescent girls positive feelings about body image, improved self-esteem, tangible experiences of competency and success, and increased self-confidence. It can also help with academic achievement.

A case could be made that participation in sports at the high school level helps a girl gain access to college and a career. Results of a 1987 survey of individuals at the executive vice-president level or above in seventy-five *Fortune* 500 companies indicated that 95 percent of those corporate executives participated in sports during high school. The February 1996 *Career World* examined the factors that really matter in gaining acceptance to a college or university. Teens who were active in sports were found to be

Westfield Memorial Library
Westfield, New Jersey

most likely to succeed at their chosen profession and make creative contributions to their community.

But the reason for taking up the sport should be much less complicated than that: You should perform gymnastics simply because you enjoy it.

1830s

Artistic gymnastics introduced to the United States by Charles Beck, Charles Follen, and Francis Lieber.

1881

The Bureau of the European Gymnastics Federation (now called the International Gymnastics Federation) formed, opening the way for international competition.

1931

Roberta C. Ranck wins the first U.S. All-Around Gymnastics Championship.

1936

U.S. women first compete in gymnastics at the Olympic Games in Berlin, Germany.

1964

Larissa Latynina completes her Olympic career in gymnastics with more medals than any athlete in Olympic history: nine gold, five silver, and four bronze.

1886

Men's gymnastics become part of the Olympics. Germany dominates the sport.

1928

The first women's gymnastic events are held at the Olympic Games. The Netherlands wins.

1960

Ukranian Larissa Latynina wins three golds, two silvers, and a bronze medal for gymnastics at the Rome Olympics.

1970

Cathy Rigby wins a silver medal in balance beam at the world championships, becoming the first American man or woman to win a medal in international gymnastics competition.

1972

Congress passes Title IX of the Educational Amendments of 1972. When President Richard Nixon signs the act on July 23, about 31,000 women are involved in college sports; spending on athletic scholarships for women is less than $100,000; and the average number of women's teams at colleges is 2.1.

Westfield Memorial Library
Westfield, New Jersey

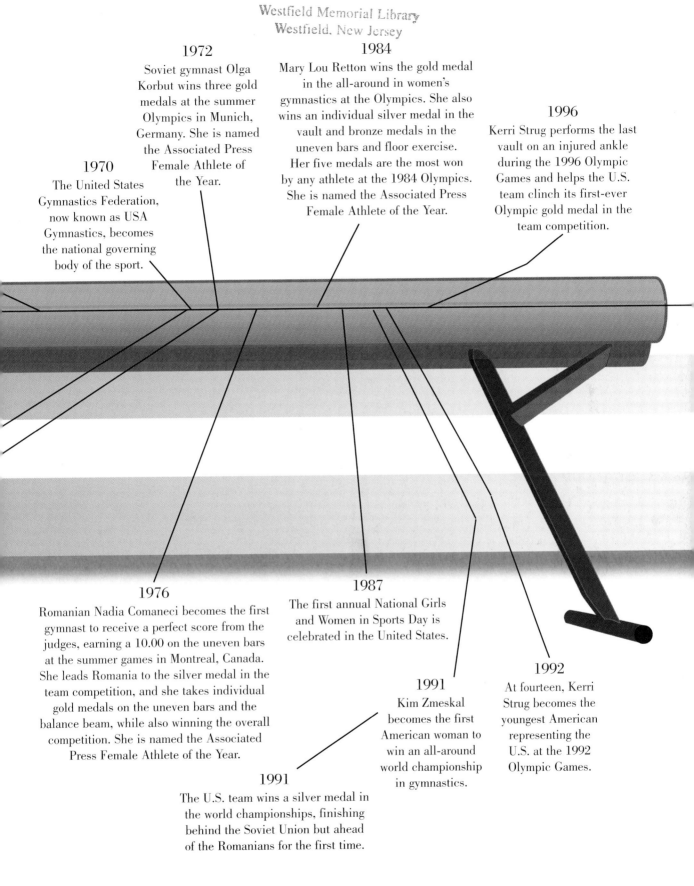

1972
Soviet gymnast Olga Korbut wins three gold medals at the summer Olympics in Munich, Germany. She is named the Associated Press Female Athlete of the Year.

1984
Mary Lou Retton wins the gold medal in the all-around in women's gymnastics at the Olympics. She also wins an individual silver medal in the vault and bronze medals in the uneven bars and floor exercise. Her five medals are the most won by any athlete at the 1984 Olympics. She is named the Associated Press Female Athlete of the Year.

1996
Kerri Strug performs the last vault on an injured ankle during the 1996 Olympic Games and helps the U.S. team clinch its first-ever Olympic gold medal in the team competition.

1970
The United States Gymnastics Federation, now known as USA Gymnastics, becomes the national governing body of the sport.

1976
Romanian Nadia Comaneci becomes the first gymnast to receive a perfect score from the judges, earning a 10.00 on the uneven bars at the summer games in Montreal, Canada. She leads Romania to the silver medal in the team competition, and she takes individual gold medals on the uneven bars and the balance beam, while also winning the overall competition. She is named the Associated Press Female Athlete of the Year.

1987
The first annual National Girls and Women in Sports Day is celebrated in the United States.

1991
Kim Zmeskal becomes the first American woman to win an all-around world championship in gymnastics.

1992
At fourteen, Kerri Strug becomes the youngest American representing the U.S. at the 1992 Olympic Games.

1991
The U.S. team wins a silver medal in the world championships, finishing behind the Soviet Union but ahead of the Romanians for the first time.

Glossary

aerial walkover   A walkover in which a gymnast rotates through the air without using her hands.

all-around gymnast   The athlete who has the highest total score on each piece of equipment.

amplitude   The greatest possible height and stretching of the body that a gymnast can achieve.

arch position   Position in which the body is curved backwards.

artistic gymnastics   The branch of gymnastics that uses four pieces of equipment and is practiced by women.

cartwheel   The move in which a gymnast turns sideways from a standing position, to a handstand, and then back to a standing position.

cast   Performed on the uneven bars, this motion involves holding the bar with on overgrip, flexing the hips at ninety degrees, and thrusting the legs back and up while extending the arms and maintaining the position.

compulsories   Set routines which contain specific movements required of all gymnasts.

dismount   To leave an apparatus at the end of a routine; usually done with flare.

elite gymnast   A gymnast who is recognized as an international competitor.

execution   The perform- ance of a routine. Form, style, and the technique used to complete the skills constitute the level of execution of an exercise.

flic-flac   Also known as a back handspring. Take off on one or two feet, jump backwards onto hands, and land on feet. This element is used in a majority of tumbling passes on the floor exercise and frequently on the balance beam.

handspring   Springing off the hands by putting the weight on the arms and using a strong push from the shoulders; can be done either forward or backward.

handstand   A movement where the gymnast balances on the hands, with the body straight above the hands.

kip   Movement from a position below the equipment to a position above.

layout position   Straight or slightly arched body position; may be seen during a movement or a still position.

optionals   Personally designed routines which show off the gymnast to her best advantage.

pike position   Body bent forward more than ninety degrees at the hips while the legs are kept straight.

pirouettes   Changing direction by twisting in the handstand position.

release   Leaving the bar to perform a move before grasping it again.

routine   A combination of stunts displaying a full range of skills on one apparatus.

salto   Flip or somersault, with the feet coming up over of the head and the body rotating around the axis the waist.

sequence   A group of movements that is part of a gymnast's routine.

somersault   Any movement in which the gymnast rotates in a full circle in the air.

spotter   Someone who stands ready to assist a gymnast if she needs help.

Westfield Memorial Library
Westfield. New Jersey

tuck   A position in which the knees and hips are bent and drawn into the chest; the body is bent at the waist.

twist   Not to be confused with a salto, a twist occurs when the gymnast rotates around the body's longitudinal axis, defined by the spine.

virtuosity   The artistry, or the degree of rhythm and harmony, displayed while a movement is executed. In general, the more flowing and seamless a series of skills appears to be, the greater the virtuosity and the higher the score.

For More Information

In the United States

Melpomene Institute
1010 University Avenue
Saint Paul, MN 55104
(651) 642-1951
e-mail: health@melpomene.org
Web site: http://www.melpomene.org
Named for a Greek woman who ran the first Olympic marathon in 1896, the Melpomene Institute helps girls and women of all ages link physical activity and health through research, publication, and education.

National Association for Girls and Women in Sport
1900 Association Drive
Reston, VA 20191-1599
(703) 476-3450
e-mail: nagws@aahperd.org

Web site: http://www.aahperd.org/nagws/nagws-main.html
Since 1899, NAGWS has championed equal funding, quality, and respect for women's sports programs.

National Collegiate Athletic Association
700 West Washington Street
P.O. Box 6222
Indianapolis, IN 46206-6222
(317) 917-6222
Web site: http://www.ncaa.org

USA Gymnastics
Pan American Plaza, Suite 300
201 S. Capitol Avenue
Indianapolis, IN 46225
(317) 237-5050
e-mail: rebound@usa-gymnastics.org
Web site: http://www.usa-gymnastics.org

Women's Sports Foundation
Eisenhower Park
East Meadow, NY 11554
(800) 227-3988
e-mail: wosport@aol.com
Web site: http://www.WomensSportsFoundation.org
The Women's Sports Foundation's mission is to promote the participation of women and girls in sports and fitness.

Westfield Memorial Library
Westfield, New Jersey

In Canada

Gymnastics Canada
5510 Canotek Road, Suite 203
Gloucester, ON K1J 9J4
(613) 748-5637
e-mail: info@gymcan.org
Web site: http://www.gymcan.org
As Canada's gymnastics federation, Gymnastics Canada is responsible for all aspects of the sport in Canada.

Seneca College of Applied Arts & Technology
(offers several courses in gymnastics)
Newnham Campus
1750 Finch Avenue East
Toronto, ON M2J 2X5
(412) 491-5050
Web site:
http://www.Senecac.on.ca
Seneca College is a
leader in educational
gymnastics in Canada
and is affiliated
with Gymnastics
Ontario and
Gymnastics
Canada.

Westfield Memorial Library
Westfield, New Jersey

Web Sites

The American Gymnastics Association
http://www.tumble.org

International Gymnastics Hall of Fame
http://www.ighof.org

The Locker Room, Sports for Kids
http://members.aol.com/msdaizy/sports/locker.html

National Collegiate Athletic Association
    Women's Gymnastics
http://www.ncaachampionships.com/gym/wgym

For Further Reading

Cohen, Joel H. *Superstars of Women's Gymnastics.*
Philadelphia: Chelsea House, 1997.

Feeney, Rik. *Gymnastics: A Guide for Parents and
Athletes.* Indianapolis, IN: Masters Press, 1995.

Gutman, Dan. *Gymnastics.* New York: Puffin
Nonfiction, 1998.

Kleinbaum, Nancy H. *The Magnificent Seven: The
Authorized Story of American Gold.* New York:
Bantam Doubleday Dell, 1996.

Lessa, Christina. *Gymnastics: Balancing Acts.*
New York: Universe Publishing, 1997.

Lovitt, Chip. *American Gymnasts: Gold Medal Dreams.*
New York: Pocket Books, 2000.

Miller, Claudia, and Gayle White. *Shannon Miller: My Child, My Hero.* Norman, OK: University of Oklahoma Press, 1999.

Miller, Shannon, and Nancy Ann Richardson. *Winning Every Day: Gold Medal Advice for a Happy, Healthy Life!* New York: Bantam Books, 1998.

Moceanu, Dominique, and Steve Woodward. *Dominique Moceanu: An American Champion—An Autobiography.* New York: Bantam Books, 1996.

Quiner, Krista. *Dominique Moceanu: A Gymnastic Sensation: A Biography.* East Hanover, NJ: Bradford Book Co., 1997.

Quiner, Krista, and Steve Lange. *Kim Zmeskal: Determination to Win: A Biography.* East Hanover, NJ: Bradford Book Co., 1995.

Quiner, Krista, and Steve Lange. *Shannon Miller: America's Most Decorated Gymnast: A Biography.* East Hanover, NJ: Bradford Book Co., 1997.

Rutledge, Rachel. *The Best of the Best in Gymnastics (Women of Sports).* Brookfield, CT: Millbrook Press, 1999.

Westfield Memorial Library
Westfield, New Jersey

Strug, Kerri, and Greg Brown. *Heart of Gold.* Dallas, TX: Taylor Publishing, 1996.

Treptow, Kurt W. *Romanian Gymnastics.* Portland, OR: Center of Romanian Studies, 1996.

USA Gymnastics. *I Can Do Gymnastics: Essential Skills for Intermediate Gymnasts.* Indianapolis, IN: Masters Press, 1993.

Index

Westfield Memorial Library
Westfield, New Jersey

Westfield Memorial Library
Westfield, New Jersey

About the Author

Ann Wesley lives and works in Bloomington, Indiana, and is an avid sports fan. She has a degree in journalism from Indiana University and has written for newspapers and magazines. Wesley currently works as a director of a Web design company.

Credits

Cover photo of gymnast © David Scott/Index Stock; cover photo of beam by Antonio Mari; pp. 3, 7, 17, 20, 22, 26, 27, 34, 49, 51, 52, 55, 56, 59, 63 by Antonio Mari; pp. 5, 9, 14, 16, 33, 37, 43 by Maura Boruchow; p. 10 © Neal Preston/Corbis; p. 13 © Bill Bachman/Index Stock; p. 28 © AFP/Corbis; p. 31 © Zephyr Picture/Index Stock; p. 38 © Reuters New Media Inc./Corbis. Diagrams on pp. 4, 46–47 by Tom Forget.

Thanks to Lynette Bernstein and the Paerdegat Gymnastic Academy.

Series Design

Danielle Goldblatt

Layout

Claudia Carlson